RECHARGE!

The Power of Praying in the Spirit

Sally Ro

(RECHARGE! The Power of Praying in the Spirit)
Copyright © 2012 by (Sally Ro)

Email: myfreshhope@gmail.com
Website: http://www.myfreshhope.com

Table of Contents

Foreword

Sally gives us practical examples from everyday life to show us the power that is released into our lives as we pray in the Holy Spirit. It is an amazing gift that God has given to the church which lies dormant in the lives of so many believers; with them failing to receive the tremendous benefits the Word of God speaks of as we let the Spirit of God pray with our spirit in the heavenly language. Way too often we believers are simply too passive in simply waiting for God to move on our behalf. *I do not write this to shame you, but to warn and counsel you as my beloved children* (1 Corinthians 4:14, Amplified Version). However, when we speak in tongues, our spirit by the Holy Spirit prays to bring God's will into our lives, our families, our workplace, our communities and our country.

Open your heart and prepare to receive as you read this inspiring book.

Pastor Duane and Jeanie Vanderklok
Resurrection Life Church/ Grandville, MI

The Refreshing

For with stammering lips and another tongue he will speak to this people, to whom he said, "This is the rest with which You may cause the weary to rest," and "THIS IS THE REFRESHING!" (Isaiah 28:11-12a).

There was a time in my life when I greatly needed refreshing. I was going through a fire that looked as if it had no signs of letting up. Actually, it wasn't a real fire, but a trial. A long trial that was leaving me, to put it simply, weary. I had begun broadcasting a television show on the TCT Christian Network in August of 2010 and after stepping out in obedience, the sparks began to fly. The scripture compares going through trials and tribulations to going through fire.

That the trial of your faith, being much more precious than of gold that perisheth, though it be tried with fire, might be found unto praise and honour and glory at the appearing of Jesus Christ (1 Peter 1:7).

The great Chicago fire, which is rumored to have been started when a cow kicked over a lantern, raged through 2,000 acres destroying 17,000 structures and tragically killing 300 people. The firemen fought for 27 hours in order to extinguish the flames. Can you imagine fighting for 27 hours? How does one feel after standing on your feet, facing a deadly inferno for that long? The answer is seemingly obvious, weary and definitely in need of refreshing.

We all go through fires and sometimes they occur back to back, one right after the other. This is what happened to me.

I made it through the first easily enough, only to discover another lurking immediately around the corner. As the intensity increased - so did my weariness. The grip on my dream was beginning to slacken. How could I continue *Fresh Hope Ministries* when my own hope was melting away? Standing so close to the flames that I could feel the heat, I heard the still, small voice of the Holy Spirit reminding me of something important. What He said enabled me to make it through. It will do the same for you. The message was short and simple:

"Pray in tongues on a consistent basis."

It was concise, to the point, and what I desperately needed to hear. Remaining strong is vital when going through the fire. I was growing weak. All because I had forgotten something: sometimes you need to put out fire with fire.

The Reason

On the day of Pentecost the disciples were gathered in the upper room when what looked to be tongues of fire came and rested upon them and they all began to speak with other tongues (Acts 2:3-4).

In bringing help for the weary, I realize it would be much more socially acceptable if I left out Pentecostal fire. Who wants to acknowledge before the world that they speak in tongues? It seems foolish, ridiculous and looking from the outside in, plum crazy. And yet, God uses the foolish things of this world to confound the wise. It stands to reason, that if one could get a look at the *"foolish things"* list, speaking in tongues is probably somewhere up near the top. I remember once, contemplating teaching about speaking in tongues for my television show, and deciding against it. I had lost sight of the immense value of this gift and therefore was hardly willing to face the persecution that would arise from endorsing this doctrinal position. Today however, I am willing. Why? It took me through the fire. It will do the same for you.

Let's read Isaiah 28:11-12 in its entirety. When we look at the end of verse 12 we will find the reason why so many are weary.

*For with stammering lips and another tongue He will speak to this people, to whom He said, "This is the rest with which You may cause the weary to rest," And, "This is the refreshing"; **Yet they would not hear.***

This same scripture is quoted by the apostle Paul in the midst of his teaching the New Testament believers about praying in tongues. Let's read it from the Young's Literal Translation.

*...in the law it hath been written, that, `With other tongues and with other lips I will speak to this people, **and not even so will they hear Me,** saith the Lord'* (I Co 14:21).

What a sad ending to both of these scriptures. *They would not hear.* Facing the fires of persecution, some have lost all strength. What is the reason? They had no desire to listen to something so foolish and utterly embarrassing as the doctrine of praying in tongues, a practice that strips us of all pride while granting true refreshing. Praying in tongues defies all earthly reason. The truth remains. *Human reasoning brings human strength.* There is a rest that comes to your inner man when you pray in tongues that defies earthly reason.

I was diagnosed with skin cancer awhile back. I did not know, at the time, it was not a serious form. When I hung up the phone after receiving the news, unrest wanted to take me over and peace began to quickly melt away in the midst of these flames. My mind began to race. As I looked at my daughters, fear raised its ugly voice, "You are going to die and they won't have a mother. You will be in heaven happy, but their hearts will break." I knew the Word of God. I knew this was not His will. The voice I was hearing was a gut wrenching lie that was attempting to burn itself into my mind and extinguish my peace completely. How could I sleep in the midst of these emotionally turbulent flames? Would I stay awake all night long, night after night, until I finally received the final test result?

While going through the fires of this life, I have not always known what or how to pray, no matter how intensely I have tried to figure it all out.

In those questioning moments I have learned to go beyond my human reasoning, open my mouth and begin to pray in a language that steps outside the natural realm and into the heavenly. It is a language that flows from the spirit, not the mind. It is a river flowing.

The King James Version says it this way:

He that believeth on me, as the scripture hath said, out of his belly shall flow rivers of living water. (John 7:38).

The water of His Word and the refreshing river of praying in the Spirit, faithfully brought me to the wonderful place of rest. Therefore, although I had been diagnosed with cancer, I was still able to sleep at night. I slept! In something as seemingly foolish as praying in tongues, I had discovered an amazing thing, *a rest that was independent of my circumstances*.

I heard.

I listened.

I walked through the flames.

I came out stronger.

For with stammering lips and another tongue He will speak to this people, to whom He said, "This is the rest with which You may cause the weary to rest," And, "This is the refreshing"; Yet they would not hear (Isaiah 28:11,12).

For this reason I pray for you. I pray you hear.

The Requirement

*And they were all **filled with the Holy Spirit and began to speak with other tongues**, as the Spirit gave them utterance.* (Acts 2:4)

Is there something that we must do in order to speak in tongues? Well, there is a requirement but it is not something that we must ***do***, it is something we must ***receive***. We must receive the fullness of the Holy Spirit. How do we receive? We ask in faith.

*"If you then, being evil, know how to give good gifts to your children, how much more will your heavenly Father give the Holy Spirit to those who **ask Him**"* (Luke 11:13)!

When I was a young girl growing up in my small home town church, the pastor one day was preaching from Ephesians 5:18.

*And do not be drunk with wine, in which is dissipation; but **be filled with the Spirit.***

I can still today, after all these years remember the impact this message had on me. When I heard this scripture my young heart cried out, "I want all of the Holy Spirit I can possibly have!" Greatly longing to be filled, I listened intently as the man of God continued to open up the scriptures in order to reveal the need of all men to be completely, utterly, and totally filled with the precious Holy Spirit.

The Spirit longs to saturate us completely, not just once, but on a continual, ongoing, never ending basis. The point that was made by my pastor that day, a point that brought me great concern, was that we could quench and thereby grieve this precious One.

The Holy Spirit is like a fire, fire can be full and raging or it can be dying out.

Do not quench the Spirit (1 Thessalonians 5:19).

After the message that day I went home and while sitting on my childhood canopy bed, I examined my heart. Had I ever truly sought His fullness with all my heart? In ignoring Him, had I quenched his power in my life? A synonym for quench is to extinguish. Would I be satisfied with lukewarm when I could have blazing hot? No, I wanted all of him. I emphatically prayed a prayer that I meant with all my heart.

Dear Father God,

I am sorry for having quenched your Holy Spirit.

I want all of the Holy Spirit I can possibly have.

Please fill me now with all the fullness of your Holy Spirit.

In Jesus Name, Amen

I had never heard anyone teach about being "*baptized*" with the Holy Spirit, yet I now understand that this is what happened to me that day. The day everything changed.

John answered, saying to all, "I indeed baptize you with water; but One mightier than I is coming, whose sandal strap I am not worthy to loose. ***He will baptize you with the Holy Spirit and fire*** (Luke 3:16).

In Acts 19 we read about some believers that had received Jesus as their Lord and Savior but had never received the fullness of the Holy Spirit. As soon as Paul realized this he prayed for them to receive. He didn't say, "Well it's good enough that you're a Christian." No, he knew the requirement.

And it happened, while Apollos was at Corinth, that Paul, having passed through the upper regions, came to Ephesus. And finding some disciples he said to them, **"Did you receive the Holy Spirit when you believed?"** *So they said to him, "We have not so much as heard whether there is a Holy Spirit."... And when Paul had laid hands on them,* **the Holy Spirit came upon them, and they spoke with tongues** *and prophesied* (Acts 19:1-2, 6).

What is required for a life of power?

"But you shall receive power when the Holy Spirit has come upon you; and you shall be witnesses to Me in Jerusalem, and in all Judea and Samaria, and to the end of the earth"*(Acts 1:8).

It could be that in reading this you have thought of some areas that you may have quenched the Holy Spirit or maybe you have recognized that you have never even asked to be filled with the Holy Spirit. I encourage you right now to pray the prayer I prayed. Ask Jesus to baptize you with His Holy Spirit. He will. That is all that is required to pray in a language that is perfect and full of power.

...and you shall receive the gift of the Holy Spirit. For the promise is to you and to your children, and to all who are afar off, as many as the Lord our God will call (Acts 2:38-39)

The promise is yours.

The Realization

*And those of the circumcision who believed were astonished, as many as came with Peter, **because the gift of the Holy Spirit had been poured out on the Gentiles also. For they heard them speak with tongues and magnify God** (Acts 10:45-46).*

As a young teen age girl I had never once heard anyone teach that we could pray in tongues today, only the opposite. Having read and studied the book of Acts, I was well aware of the fact that New Testament believers prayed in tongues after they received the Holy Spirit; but that was then and this was now. The same pastor who taught me to be filled with the Holy Spirit also taught, quite convincingly, that tongues were not for today. I believed everything he said.

I can clearly remember one sermon in particular. *"Tongues are not for today. They have ceased, passed away,"* he declared. To prove his point, he assertively read 1 Corinthians 13:8. Just the way he read it, brought me to the realization that he believed it with all his heart.

*Love never fails. But whether there are prophecies, they will fail; **whether there are tongues, they will cease;** whether there is knowledge, it will vanish away* (1 Corinthians 13:8).

There it was in black and white, written in the infallible Word of God Almighty. In order to leave absolutely no room for doubt whether this possibly was still future tense, he quickly read 1 Corinthians 13:11.

*But when that which is **perfect** has come, then that which is in part will be done away (1 Corinthians 13:10).*

13

The Bible is perfect. Therefore, he reasoned, the perfect referred to here in this scripture is the Bible, the perfect Word of God. *"Tongues ceased, he firmly stated, when the Bible was completely written."* I knew the Bible was perfect and so, I easily believed everything he said. Never once would I attempt to pray in tongues. To do so, in my reasoning, would be completely and totally wrong.

Until, I faced the fire.

A fire that was so painful I didn't know how to pray.

Have you ever been there?

How do you pray when you don't know what to pray? In the midst of my questionings, God led me by His Spirit, to His Word and I came face to face with a realization that shattered my previous conviction and enabled me to do something amazing: pray the perfect will of God.

Likewise the Spirit also helps in our weaknesses. **For we do not know what we should pray for as we ought, but** *the Spirit Himself makes intercession for us with groanings which cannot be uttered.* (Romans 8:26).

Allow me to tell you about that day, the day of my realization.

It was years later and I was reading 1 Corinthians 13:8 once again. As I did, I remembered clearly the sermon I had heard concerning this scripture, and the firm declaration that was made - the perfect is the Bible. Not stopping at verse 8, I continued reading right on through to the end of the chapter. All of a sudden, my spiritual eyes were opened and I realized something for the very first time… *the state of full perfection would not arrive until we see Jesus face to face at the time of the final redemption.*

14

When every knee bows and the new heaven and earth come into manifestation, **then all will be perfect**. Until then, imperfection will live among us. Spiritual gifts will no longer be needed in heaven. Tongues, prophecy, words of wisdom and knowledge will pass away when the kingdom of God comes into full manifestation. Then we shall know, just as we are known. These gifts that help us see in part will no longer be needed, for then we shall see clearly. The one thing that will remain is love. Love will never cease, it will never pass away. This is why love is the greatest. It will never fail.

Love will fill heaven, for God is love.

*Love never fails. But whether there are prophecies, they will fail; whether there are tongues, they will cease; whether there is knowledge, it will vanish away. For we know in part and we prophesy in part. But **when that which is perfect has come, then that which is in part will be done away**. When I was a child, I spoke as a child, I understood as a child, I thought as a child; but when I became a man, I put away childish things. **For now we see in a mirror, dimly, but then face to face. Now I know in part, but then I shall know just as I also am known**. And now abide faith, hope, love, these three; but the greatest of these is love* (1 Corinthians 13:8-13).

All of a sudden, I realized for the first time, spiritual gifts were not needed in heaven, but oh, how desperately they were needed on this earth! Until I saw Jesus face to face, I needed help in prayer. Of all this, I was thoroughly convinced. What did I do in the face of this revelation?

I opened my mouth and prayed in tongues.

The Reaction

*"And these signs will follow **those who believe**: In My name they will cast out demons; **they will speak with new tongues**"* (Mark 16:17)

My reaction, after hearing myself begin to pray in tongues, was to immediately turn around and stare at myself in the mirror, watching in amazement as this wonderful, new heavenly language spilled from my lips. I was astonished, thrilled, and overjoyed. I knew I was praying beyond myself, praying the perfect will of God, I truly rejoiced, knowing I had just experienced a significant breakthrough in my spiritual life.

As I continued to stare at myself, praying, the phone rang. It was my husband, Mark. I immediately shared with him my exciting news. It is funny, when I think of it, how mild his reaction was. The apparent lack of enthusiasm did not put a damper on my flame. His calm met my excitement as I quickly rattled off my surprising news.

"Guess, what I just did?

"What?"

"I prayed in tongues!!!!"

"Oh."

In the upcoming days ahead, I eagerly set to work explaining to my husband how wonderful a gift I had received. The truth is, however, he was not immediately convinced that speaking in new tongues was God willed for everyone.

Like me, it took time in the Word, for him to discover for himself that yes, it was God's will for **all** believers to speak in tongues. In attempting to share this gift with others I have faced this reaction more than once: *the gift of tongues is not for me. It may be for others, but it is not for me.*

My computer is a great asset to me when I study. It brings the world to my fingertips, broadens my horizons and just plain makes my life easier. The first computer that I ever owned, however, was given to me because I did not want to spend my own money on something that I believed would be hard to learn and of little value to my life. To this day, I can still remember the man who gave me the computer, telling me how wonderful it would be to have one and what a great help it would be to me. Still not a hundred percent convinced, he talked me into giving it a try- and oh, I am so glad he did! My computer has become, not just a help in my life, but also a major tool in my ministry. Where would I be if I had remained convinced that computers were for some people but not for me? I would not be producing a weekly television program that is for sure. May I be your friend today? May I convince you that speaking in other tongues is something everyone needs? You may have never tried to speak in tongues before, just like I had never tried to work a computer, but oh, if you will give it a try, it will not just be a help in your life – it will be great help. It will...

- help you to overcome this imperfect world.

- help you to laugh and enjoy life.

- help you to be free from worry and walk in peace.

- help you to pray beyond yourself

In truth, the words "help you" are an understatement.

17

I am spending much time working on this book. I could be taking it easy. Instead, I am sitting here, when it is nice outside, writing. Writing to you, writing because I know the value of this gift is priceless. My great desire is to see you speak in tongues.

The Apostle Paul writing to you as well, by inspiration of the Holy Spirit, felt the same burning. His words carry much more weight than mine, for the words He wrote were in actual truth, the inspired Words of God.

Look at Paul's great desire:

*Now **I desire** that ye should **all** speak with tongues...*

(1 Corinthians 14:5/ Darby's Translation)

*Now **I would like every one of you** to speak in tongues...*

(1 Corinthians 14:5/New International Version)

What more do you need? Paul made it clear. God desires all of us to speak with tongues. If you still need convincing that speaking in tongues is a gift for all, let's take a closer look at the scriptures. The Bible clearly states, *"by the mouth of two or three witnesses every word may be established"* (Matthew 18:16). Let us together examine three different witnesses in order to establish the truth.

The First Witness Is Paul:

*Now I want you **all** to speak in tongues...* (1 Corinthians 14:5).

*Therefore if the whole church comes together in one place and **all** speak with tongues...* (1 Corinthians 14:23).

The Second Witness Is Mark:

*"And these signs will follow **those who believe**: In My name they will cast out demons; **they will speak with new tongues**"* (Mark 16:17).

The Third Witness Is Luke:

*And they were **all** filled with the Holy Spirit and **began to speak with other tongues,** as the Spirit gave them utterance......and you shall receive the gift of the Holy Spirit. For the promise is to you and to your children, **and to all who are afar off, as many as the Lord our God will call*** (Acts 2:4, 38b-39).

While we are at it, let's add a fourth witness.

The Witness of the Early Church:

Throughout the book of Acts there is a consistent pattern of all believers who were filled with the Holy Spirit speaking in tongues. We also see, through the writings of the early church fathers who lived after all the apostles who wrote the Bible had died, such as Irenaeus and Augustine of Hippo, how speaking in tongues was still an important part of the early church believer's life. There is also written evidence of the early church martyrs (A.D. 300) singing and speaking in unknown tongues as they faced the ultimate fire of persecution.

Don't take my word for it,

- take God's.

19

The Rebuttal

Some will argue with me and say,

"Yes, but look what it says in 1 Corinthians ...

*for to one is given the word of wisdom through the Spirit, to another the word of knowledge through the same Spirit, to another faith by the same Spirit, to another gifts of healings by the same Spirit, to another the working of miracles, to another prophecy, to another discerning of spirits, **to another different kinds of tongues**, to another the interpretation of tongues. But one and the same Spirit works all these things, **distributing to each one individually as He wills*** (1 Corinthians 12:8-11).

*And in 1 Corinthians 12:30: Do all have gifts of healings? **Do all speak with tongues?** Do all interpret?*

*See...there it is, in black in white, God gives **some** the ability to speak in tongues not **all**."*

Those who would make this claim should understand that First Corinthians 12 is not the only scripture written concerning the gift of tongues and that when we take all the scriptures concerning this subject together, examining them as a whole, it is easy to understand that the gift of tongues can be placed in two different categories.

1. Private Tongues

    -a gift given to ALL believers

2. Public Tongues

    -a gift given to SOME believers

20

It is made clear in the scriptures that there are some who possess the wonderful gift of speaking in tongues in a public setting, such as a church service. Like all of the gifts of the Spirit, it is to operate decently and in order. Direction is given that in a public gathering no more than three people should speak in tongues and the tongues must be interpreted in English in order to edify, comfort and exhort those who hear it.

If anyone speaks in a tongue, let there be two or at the most three, each in turn, and let one interpret (1 Corinthians 14:27).

I, for one, am so glad that the gift of speaking in tongues and seeing those tongues interpreted has been given, because the operation of this gift has been a source of amazing strength, supernatural comfort and faith building guidance in my life. I have seen it flow with such accuracy and anointing, it was as if the one who gave the message in tongues had read the pastor's notes before he gave the sermon! It increases the faith of all the believers when God reveals what the pastor is about to preach before he has yet spoken one word.

My heart is grieved when I think of the many churches that are not open to this gift. The gift of speaking in tongues contains much power – power, that I, myself, have often desperately needed to tap into.

For example, in the early days of my television ministry, I was facing some hard times. During this season, a powerful woman of God spoke over me in tongues during a church service and then immediately interpreted what she had prayed. She prophesied that I would expand my television ministry beyond the one station I was currently on and possess all the money I needed in order to do it.

21

This was the deep desire of my heart, and hearing it spoken forth by the Spirit greatly increased my faith. I am filled with thankfulness to report that it has come to pass just as she said! Today I am currently on six stations and every month the money I need to keep going is always there.

She went on to speak other words of encouragement. I wrote it all down and just now while writing this I paused, took it out, and read it all once more. It has been five years since this tongue and its interpretation were first given to me, and I still find hope, faith and encouragement as I read it....five years later! I am edified. I am comforted. I am built up. Five years later, these words still possess the amazing power to do all that! This is why I fight for the gifts of prophecy, tongues and the interpretation of tongues - they amplify hope and increase our faith. How could they not, for in truth, they are the very voice of God.

His voice will lead us through any fire, no matter how hot.

As wonderful and awesome as the gift of praying publicly in tongues is, only *some* believers possess it. The gift of praying in tongues in our prayer life however, is available to *all* believers who possess the *will* to do it. This is why the Apostle Paul said,

What is the conclusion then? ***I will pray with the spirit, and I will*** *also pray with the understanding* (1 Corinthians 14:15).

I have made the point that we must have the *will* for it because the sad truth is that many believers do not. Take for example a young man I once knew whose life was filled with unnecessary weakness, pain and confusion. It came to my attention that he believed that only a few believers could pray in tongues and he was not one of them. Yet, when I tried to show him the scriptures that would confirm that it was indeed God's will for all believers to pray in tongues, it became quite evident to me that he did not really desire the gift.

Refusing to give up, I endeavored to give him an excellent audio teaching on this subject. Although he had told me he wanted to pray in tongues, whenever I asked him if he had listened to the teaching he would always say, "I have been too busy." I asked again and again, but no matter how hard I tried- I could never get him to listen.

*It is said in the Law-'In strange tongues and by the lips of strangers will I speak to this people, **but even then they will not listen to me,** says the Lord'* (1 Corinthians 14:21 – Twentieth Century New Testament).

Was he really "too busy" or did he simply not possess the desire or will to receive? Had he, on purpose, refused to listen?

Praying in tongues involves our will – our will to listen.

The Rebuilding

I was online the other day and read about a workout plan that claims to have the ability to rebuild your body in just five short weeks! Doesn't sound too bad, huh? Another ad I spotted told how you could rebuild your body into the likes of the bionic woman. Some amazing claims for sure, but just maybe, a little too good to be true.

I have a son-in-law who is a body builder. It has taken him much longer than five weeks to get where he is today. He built up his physical body with a lot of sweat and hard work. Unfortunately, he still could not take on the bionic woman!

Our physical man can indeed be built up, made stronger. There definitely is profit that comes to us through physical exercise. This is all well and good. The truth remains, however, no matter how much we exercise it, one day this body will die, be buried and eventually rot completely away. Our spirit man, however, never dies. Our spirit lives forever. This is why, though physical exercise is good, spiritual exercise is much better. Physical exercise brings temporary profit. Spiritual exercise brings eternal profit.

For bodily exercise profits a little, but godliness is profitable for all things, having promise of the life that now is and of that which is to come (1 Timothy 4:8).

I have been a Christian for many years, over forty. Through those years I have seen many men and women of God, who I thought were spiritually strong, fall into gross temptation. As I write, I am reminded of one couple that my husband and I use to spend time with, laughing and hanging out together. They appeared to be such strong Christians with the perfect marriage.

I remember overhearing the husband compliment his wife quite often. Saying things like, *"You are so beautiful. Your hair is so nice...etc...etc."* They were huggy, squeezy all the time. When I saw and heard all this, I thought, *"They must have the perfect marriage."* My husband and I were not quite so affectionate in public and we didn't always ooze over with compliments for one another. In my mind I began to think that somehow they had topped us in the marriage category. I was tempted to be envious - the perfect marriage and they had achieved it. What I have discovered through the years, however, is that looks can be quite deceiving. On the outside we can look so good, but if on the inside our spirit man has not been edified, we can miss the perfect will of God for our life, for our marriage.

I can still remember the shock I felt when I heard that this couple was getting a divorce. "No way," I thought, "They are strong committed Christians with an almost perfect love for each other!" I was wrong in my assumption that they were both strong. The husband had neglected to exercise his spirit. As a result, he left his wife for another woman -the very wife he had oozed over, walked hand in hand in the house of God with, raised three children with, laughed with, and taken summer vacations with. How sad, how entirely sad. The husband, through neglecting his spirit, was overtaken by a dark weakness that affected his entire family –the weakness of his flesh. Let us learn from this example. Let us not forget. We are two parts – spirit and flesh. The part you exercise is the part that dominates.

A marriage controlled by the flesh is weak.

A marriage controlled by the spirit will last, forever strong.

Jesus summed it up well.

"Watch and pray, lest you enter into temptation. The spirit indeed is willing, but the flesh is weak" (Matthew 26:41).

I cannot emphasize enough the importance of keeping our spirit man stronger than our flesh. The two are in constant battle against each other. Our flesh is not redeemed at salvation, only our spirit. Flesh will only be made perfect when we see Jesus face to face at the time of the final redemption. Until then, we must crucify it - put it under - control it or it will control you. **The part you edify, spirit vs. flesh, is the part that dominates.**

Our spirit man is made perfect at the day of salvation, a new creation, fearless, hope filled, strong in faith, and completely without sin. Our flesh, on the other hand, is the old me, fearful, having little hope, lacking true faith, imperfect and easily conquered by sin. The flesh will cause you to do those things you do not want to do.

For the flesh lusts against the Spirit, and the Spirit against the flesh; and these are contrary to one another, so that you do not do the things that you wish (Galatians 5:17).

Again:
The part you edify, spirit vs. flesh, is the part that dominates.

Look carefully at the following scriptures, keeping in mind that **to edify**, by definition is to **build up** or **strengthen.** It is often defined as intellectual, moral or spiritual improvement.

*He who speaks in a tongue edifies himself (*1 Corinthians 14:4a).

*But you, beloved, **building yourselves up** on your most holy faith, praying in the Holy Spirit* (Jude 1:20).

Praying in tongues is a spiritual discipline that strengthens our spirit enabling it to easily conquer our flesh. It is not the only one, but it is perhaps, the one most neglected.

Be honest with yourself. Have you neglected it?

26

The Ring

*So the child grew and **became strong in spirit**, and was in the deserts till the day of his manifestation to Israel* (Luke 1:80).

Sometimes my spiritual life has reminded me of the *Rocky* movie. Do you remember at the end of the movie when Rocky kept getting knocked down again and again and again? His face went from baby porcelain smooth to bloody, raw red in the process and it looked like there was no way that he would have the strength to get up again. I have felt this way sometimes, running into the fist of one trial right after the other until I was left feeling numb and about ready to pass out. Times like these require a supernatural recharge in order to get up again before the final countdown.

We are hard pressed on every side, yet not crushed; we are perplexed, but not in despair; persecuted, but not forsaken; struck down, but not destroyed-- always carrying about in the body the dying of the Lord Jesus, that the life of Jesus also may be manifested in our body (2 Corinthians 4:8-10).

The force of a fire coming at you from every side can knock you off your feet. When your gut is wrenching, your knees feel like rubber and all you want to do is lay flat on the mat – physical strength cannot get you up again, only supernatural. The fight of faith necessitates the training and strengthening of our spirit. Why?

Flesh is consumed by the flames. Spirit gets up again.

I once faced the searing flames of rejection. It was not the first blaze of this nature that I had faced, but in truth it may have hurt the most. Why? It was not just a fire – it was *a ring of fire.*

Some fires do more damage than others. For example, when people turn against us that we don't know real well, though we may not cherish the rejection, the pain is only skin deep. Being rejected by people who are significant in our life however, is a flame that burns a little deeper. When we find ourselves rejected by multiple people who are significant in our life - the flames go deeper still. It is a ring of fire that presses from every side.

The apostle Paul was rejected again and again by those he loved. Persecution came at him from every side.

*We are **hard pressed on every side** (2 Corinthians 4:8a).*

It was the position I was in, having been rejected by, not just one – but by many who were significant to me. In the middle of it all, I remember getting on my bike and riding aimlessly down an old country road. Riding silently behind a timeworn city hall, I discovered a secret place where I could stand alone. That is what I did, just stood there gazing emptily at the trees that hemmed me in. My tears had long dried. I was at the place called numbness. It is not a fun place to be, the place where you are shutting down your emotions. Dazed and confused, my physical body was standing there looking up into the treetops, but my soul was lying ever so still on the mat. The punches had been delivered by the hands of those I had loved which made it all hurt so much more. King David once felt these blows as well.

If an enemy were insulting me, I could endure it; if a foe were raising himself against me, I could hide from him. But it is you, a man like myself, my companion, my close friend, with whom I once enjoyed sweet fellowship as we walked with the throng at the house of God. (Psalm 55:12-14 – NIV).

I am so thankful that I had reached a firm conclusion long before I went through this inferno.

What is the conclusion then? **I will pray with the spirit,** *and I will also pray with the understanding.* **I will sing with the spirit,** *and I will also sing with the understanding* (I Corinthians 14:15).

Many times in my life I have not only prayed in tongues, I have also opened my mouth and sang in tongues. When trapped by a ring of fire, rescue will often come to us in a song. It provides a place to hide, a place to heal - a place to feel again.

You are my hiding place; You shall preserve me from trouble; You shall surround me with songs of deliverance (Psalm 32:7).

This is why I urge you to pray and sing in tongues; but ***don't stop there.*** After you have prayed, ask God to allow you to *interpret the tongues* you have spoken. Remember, we can ALL flow in the gifts of the spirit in our personal lives. We may not all interpret tongues in the church service, but if we pray and ask God, He will allow us to interpret the tongues we have spoken in our personal life.

Therefore let him who speaks in a tongue pray that he may interpret. (1 Corinthians 14:13).

It is very important for you to pray for the interpretation to the tongues that you speak. Why? **The interpretation will often keep you from being crushed.**

We are hard pressed on every side, ***yet not crushed...***
(1 Corinthians 4:8)

I had begun to shut off my emotions in order to find release from the crushing that was taking place in my heart. When all of a sudden, something happened – an interpretation filled my mouth.

In the midst of my solitude, still staring up at the treetops, I did something startling. Lifting my bruised and broken voice, I began to sing – a song not of the flesh but of the spirit. I sang against the heaviness and as I did, something stunning happened.

The song lifted me above the crushing.

My heart was liberated as I sang of a place rejection could never enter - my place in Him. I had been on a long journey, if you will, looking for a place to belong. Where did I belong? I belonged with Him. I belonged with Him! I sang it over and over, and as I did something miraculous happened. The paralyzing numbness let go of my heart as hot tears rushed sweetly down my cheeks. I was able to feel again.

The interpretation of my tongues allowed me to see something clearly, something I thought I already knew but had never really grasped. Many people had walked away from me and though I no longer felt safely "at home" with them – my home sweet home would forever be with my Jesus. He was with me. He would never leave me. He would never forsake me. He would never close the door and shut me out. Growing up in the church I should have already known this. The truth is, however, that we can know something with our mind but never interpret it fully with our heart. One of the definitions of the word interpret is to *discover the meaning.* Revelation is the opening of our eyes to spiritual truths. It enables us to see what we never really saw before. The interpretation of tongues enabled me to find the place where I belonged.

Therefore let him who speaks in a tongue pray that he may interpret. (1 Corinthians 14:13).

Why? It opens your eyes.

The Revelation

*There are, it may be, **so many kinds of voices in the world**, and none of them is unmeaning, if, then, I do not know the power of the voice, I shall be to him who is speaking a foreigner, and he who is speaking, is to me a foreigner; so also ye, since ye are earnestly desirous of spiritual gifts, for the building up of the assembly seek that ye may abound; wherefore he who is speaking in an unknown tongue--**let him pray that he may interpret*** (1 Corinthians 14:10-13 – Young's Literal Translation).

It is always good to have someone in your corner when you are in the middle of the ring. Rocky had Mickey, his rough, fiery trainer who never let him quit. His voice was tough, raspy and easy to recognize. When directing Rocky in the heat of the fight it was easy to hear his voice above the crowd.

In the midst of our fight many voices will attempt to direct us. Some are yelling, "Give up!" Others scream, "Throw in the towel!" Mockers yell, "You're going down for the count!" There is a still, small voice, however, that says, "Keep going. Hold on. The victory is yours." It is the voice of God. At times it can be easy to miss it in the crowd. His voice cannot be heard with ears of the flesh, only with ears of the spirit. This is another reason why we need to pray in tongues on a consistent basis. Praying in tongues enables us to hear and recognize His voice.

The interpretation of tongues amplifies it further still.

tongues + the interpretation of tongues = prophecy

Think of it like this, two ten dollar bills equal the same as one twenty dollar bill. They may be completely different but the sum is identical.

The Apostle Paul said that if you speak in tongues in a public service make sure you interpret them. Why? The two together bring the voice of God to the entire assembly.

...for he who prophesies is greater than he who speaks with tongues, unless indeed he interprets, that the church may receive edification (1 Corinthians 14:5b).

Sitting here at my computer I just now thought of a time I was in a church service as a young girl. A lady stood up and began to speak loudly in tongues, all the while shaking her hand in a violent manner as she did. To the best of my recollection, there was no interpretation. All I can remember is the tongues that were screamed out. I had no idea what was going on. It did not edify me, it only confused me. This is why, in public, we need to interpret the tongues we pray so that everyone is edified and helped. Unbelievers will be more confused than anybody if no interpretation is given and will probably leave the gathering thinking we Christians are all a little nutsy.

*Therefore if the whole church comes together in one place and all speak with tongues, and there come in those who are uninformed or unbelievers, will they not say that you are out of your mind? But if all prophesy, and an unbeliever or an uninformed person comes in, he is convinced by all, he is convicted by all. And thus **the secrets of his heart are revealed;** and so, falling down on his face, he will worship God and report that God is truly among you* (1 Corinthians 14:23-25).

The above scripture makes is clear. Prophesy reveals secrets. Things only God knows about. It can even reveal secrets of the future, secrets that deliver us in the day of famine.

... Agabus, stood up and showed by the Spirit that there was going to be a great famine throughout all the world, which also happened in the days of Claudius Caesar (Acts 11:28).

Many times while praying in tongues, I will see someone with what I call—the eyes of my spirit. I don't literally see them in real life; a picture of them comes to my heart as I am praying. I am able to see them in my sanctified imagination.

And a vision appeared to Paul in the night. A man of Macedonia stood and pleaded with him, saying, "Come over to Macedonia and help us" (Acts 16:9).

Often, this is God allowing me to interpret who I am praying for in tongues. At times He reveals specific things I should pray concerning them. Today as I was talking on the phone to my oldest daughter, Sasha, I was reminded of a specific morning when the gift of interpreting tongues in my personal prayer life was, and I am not overstating it—priceless.

It was a special morning because this was the day that Sasha was driving home from college in order to spend Christmas with the family. She was bringing with her someone for us to meet for the first time, a young man named Jay Douglas. In the natural, I should have felt nothing but excitement, but the opposite occurred. I sensed the need to pray. The still, small voice of God was clearly directing me to pray specifically for Sasha and Jay, as with the eyes of my spirit I saw them driving home in their SUV. I prayed with my understanding, praying that God would protect their physical bodies from all harm as they drove home. I decreed and declared that the angels of God were sent to protect them. Yes, I prayed with the understanding yet; I also prayed fervently with the spirit. My intercession began to deepen. It plunged to a depth that was so immense my prayer became nothing less than a literal groan.

A secret was being prayed out.

Likewise the Spirit also helps in our weaknesses. For we do not know what we should pray for as we ought, but the Spirit Himself makes intercession for us with groanings which cannot be uttered (Romans 8:26).

I prayed until I felt a release come, declaring, "In Jesus Name, Amen!" A short time later I received a phone call. It was Sasha. She had been driving while Jay slept in the backseat– when all of a sudden they encountered black ice. The ice caused them to slide some distance across the expressway, flip completely over and finally land upside down. The vehicle was totaled. They, on the other hand, were kept completely safe and unharmed.

This, my friend, is the power of secrets being revealed.

I exhort you to take heed to what the apostle Paul said:

Therefore, brethren, desire earnestly to prophesy, and do not forbid to speak with tongues (1 Corinthians 14:39).

The young man I met that day for the first time, Jay Douglas, is today my son-in-law. I am so thankful they were not seriously injured that day. Sasha and Jay have successfully made my husband and I, grandpa and grandma for the first time. We are so blessed with our precious granddaughter, Boston Rose.

Think about it for a minute. When we are praying in the spirit for someone, our intercession definitely helps them on an individual basis—but the power does not stop there! Praying in the spirit has the tremendous ability of reaching far into the future and blessing the lineage to come! That, my friend, is amazing.

I thank my God I speak with tongues more than you all...

(1 Corinthians 14:18).

The Rooting

*For this reason I bow my knees to the Father of our Lord Jesus Christ, from whom the whole family in heaven and earth is named, that He would grant you, according to the riches of His glory, **to be strengthened with might through His Spirit in the inner man,** that Christ may dwell in your hearts through faith; that you, **being rooted and grounded in love**...*
(Ephesians 3:14-17)

In this powerful prayer Paul prays for our inner man, which is our spirit, to be strengthened and rooted in love. Praying in tongues strengthens and edifies your spirit man.

*He who speaks in a tongue **edifies** himself (*1 Corinthians 14:4a).

When our spirit is stronger than our flesh we remain rooted and grounded in unconditional love. We stay in love regardless of the circumstances. However, when our flesh reigns, love is forever and only conditional. If the conditions are not right, our love is easily uprooted. Praying in tongues will help keep us rooted in the love of God. It will empower us to overcome those sins which would so easily entangle us.

All of the commandments are fulfilled in perfect love.

Then one of them, a lawyer, asked Him a question, testing Him, and saying, "Teacher, which is the great commandment in the law?" Jesus said to him," 'You shall love the Lord your God with all your heart, with all your soul, and with all your mind.' This is the first and great commandment. And the second is like it: 'You shall love your neighbor as yourself.' On these two commandments hang all the Law and the Prophets" (Matthew 22:35-40).

Our spirit man always walks in perfect love. So it stands to reason that if praying in tongues edifies our spirit, it also keeps us in the love of God! Look at how Jude forms the progressive pattern of building yourself up by praying in the Holy Spirit, which will then lead to your continuing in the love of God.

But you, beloved, building yourselves up on your most holy faith, praying in the Holy Spirit, keep yourselves in the love of God (Jude 20,21a).

Is there any weight or sin in your life that you are having a hard time getting rid of? God can use something as "foolish" as praying in tongues to help set you free. In fact, before I first started praying in tongues I was addicted to reading love stories that were not always as "clean" as they should be. Although they were a sin and a weight in my life that was entangling me and hindering my Christian race, I could not seem to let them go. I would rationalize my reasons for reading them to myself. The good news— after I began to pray in tongues, I successfully developed the strength of spirit needed in order to pry my hands of flesh off those books! When I look back at my life it is very easy to see the tremendous difference that occurred in my life after fully utilizing the gift of praying in tongues. I had a power to overcome sin that I did not possess before.

...strengthened with all might, according to His glorious power, for all patience and longsuffering with joy (Colossians 1:11)

How do we stay rooted in love when suffering long? Open your mouth and pray in tongues. As you do, your love is perfected and you are able to face the hottest flames of tribulation, fearless.

There is no fear in love; but perfect love casts out fear, because fear involves torment. But he who fears has not been made perfect in love (1 John 4:18).

The fire faced with fear will melt us.

The fire faced with faith makes us stronger.

This is why it is important to pray in tongues when we encounter fear in our lives. Eyes of the flesh are terrified when they see the flames. Eyes of the spirit perceive the love of God and rest in the flames, knowing a loving God is working it all together for their good. His love will not allow the flames to consume us, only to strengthen us. ***Remember, the hottest fire makes the hardest steel.***

...quenched the violence of fire, escaped the edge of the sword, out of weakness were made strong (Hebrews 11:34).

Fire can burn at different temperatures. A candle burns at roughly 1800° F, while ox hydrogen can burn at 3600° F and above. Some fires we face are hotter than others. My husband losing a job he had worked at for over twenty years, for example, was a very hot blaze. We were not the first to encounter intense heat. Three Hebrew children, named Shadrach, Meshach and Abed-nego had walked through a furnace turned up seven times hotter than usual.

*Then Nebuchadnezzar was full of fury, and the expression on his face changed toward Shadrach, Meshach, and Abed-Nego. He spoke and commanded that they **heat the furnace seven times more than it was usually heated**. And he commanded certain mighty men of valor who were in his army to bind Shadrach, Meshach, and Abed-Nego, and cast them into the burning fiery furnace. Then these men were bound in their coats, their trousers, their turbans, and their other garments, and were cast into the midst of the burning fiery furnace.* (Daniel 3:19-21).

Q: How do we walk through a fire this hot?

A: *I say then:* **Walk in the Spirit** (Galatians 5:16).

The same inferno which destroys the flesh strengthens the spirit.

When my husband lost his job I continued to pray in tongues. I was determined—determined to walk through by the spirit. One day while praying I saw the most amazing thing. I saw myself walking down a road; but I was not alone. Jesus was walking with me. He was walking close to me, right by my side. And so, yes, my husband had lost his job. Yes, we had bills that needed to be paid. Yes, it was not easy. But the biggest and far greatest yes remained. *Yes, Jesus was walking with me in the midst of the fire.* I saw the love of God in the midst of the flames. It caused my faith to grow.

...but faith which worketh by love (Galatians 5:6).

After King Nebuchadnezzar threw the three Hebrew children into the flames he took a peek inside the furnace to see the damage that was done. There was nothing to see. No damage had been done. The fire had not even singed a single hair on their heads! They had fallen into the fire **bound.**

...fell down bound into the midst of the burning fiery furnace (Daniel 3:23b).

The amazing this is, the only thing that burned in the fire were the ropes that bound them! They were now completely **loose**! Loose and walking free in the fire. And what's more, they were not alone. There was a fourth man walking with them through the fire.

"Look!" he answered, *"I see four men loose, walking in the midst of the fire; and they are not hurt, and the form of the fourth is like the Son of God."* (Daniel 3:25).

I was now finally able to see through the smoke. The flames could not hurt me. I was with Jesus. Jesus was with me! In the face of this revelation I opened my mouth and began to sing a spontaneous song of the spirit:

Here in this place I can do anything.

Here in this place my needs are supplied.

Here in this place favor makes a way for me.

Here in this place, right here, by Your side.

In the wake of this powerful revelation, favor soon made a way for a new job to come through! Now, when I think of the great fear that gripped my heart when my husband first lost his job and how I was literally weeping and thinking, "Oh no, I am going to need to quit the ministry and find a job that will help us pay the bills." I realize how much I learned in the heart of this fire. I learned to trust. I learned He would never leave me. I learned He was faithful to His Word. My faith in His love and care for us had literally strengthened in the flames. The only thing consumed was the fear that had bound me.

When facing your hottest fire, open your mouth and pray in tongues. As you do, your spirit is rooted in the love of God to such a degree, it no longer matters how hot the flames – *you just look up and smile at the Fourth Man in the fire, and everything that binds you simply burns away.*

The Revealing

Whom will he teach knowledge? And whom will he make to understand the message? ...For with stammering lips and another tongue He will speak to this people (Isaiah 28:9a, 11).

After I received the baptism of the Holy Spirit and began to pray in tongues, I was able to understand the Bible in a way that I had never understood it before. At times it seemed as if the words on the page were leaping out at me in 3-D, like I was seeing a scripture for the very first time, even though I had already read it numerous times before. My eyes were opened in a new way, illumined if you will. Now sometimes, when I read the Bible, passages that I had never really understood before were suddenly revealed to me. Praying in the Spirit, the Spirit of Truth, resulted in truth being revealed to me.

However, when He, the Spirit of truth, has come, He will guide you into all truth... (John 16:13a).

There is a big difference between simple knowledge and revelation knowledge! When we pray in tongues our spirit is edified. Edification of our spirit man will always result in a better understanding of the Word of God. Why? Because only our born again, recreated spirit man is renewed in knowledge and able to fully grasp the truth of God's Word. Our flesh forever remains clueless.

...and have put on the new man who is renewed in knowledge according to the image of Him who created him (Colossians 3:10).

I have heard that there are 365 verses in the Bible that address the topic of fear. There are also quite a number that tell us not to worry. Even so, I was still bound by both – fear and worry. It was not until I began praying in tongues that I began to be set free from this deadly duo. I had been reading the black and white print on the page concerning fear with eyes of the flesh. However, I needed enlightened eyes of the spirit in order to clearly perceive truth. Take for example the following well known scripture.

Be anxious for nothing, but in everything by prayer and supplication, with thanksgiving, let your requests be made known to God (Philippians 4:6).

Plain and simple, don't be anxious. Yet, one night here I was, doing it again - worrying. I cannot remember clearly what sort of devouring fire I was restless about, but I do remember it was keeping me awake. I had probably read Philippians 4:6 over a hundred times in my life. Now, as I tossed in bed, it came strongly to my mind once again. Only this time, it was as if two of the words in this scripture were highlighted boldly in my thoughts.

*Be anxious for **nothing**, but in **everything** by prayer and supplication, with thanksgiving, let your requests be made known to God* (Philippians 4:6).

Nothing and everything, those two simple words, were revealed to me in a way I had never seen them before. There was **nothing, absolutely nothing** to worry about. **Everything, absolutely everything** was covered by prayer. My striving ceased as truth revealed produced rest in my heart. I fell asleep.

Nothing could devour me. Everything was o.k.

41

The Release

...if we ask anything according to His will, He hears us. And if we know that He hears us, whatever we ask, we know that we have the petitions that we have asked of Him (1 John 5:14, 15).

Why pray? Doesn't God's will automatically just take place anyway? I am about to write something that may shock a lot of people - ***God's will does not always take place.*** Yes, I will say it again; God's will does not always take place. Let me show you what I mean in three different ways.

First of all, the scripture makes is clear that God is not willing for any to perish and for all to come to repentance. Yet, every day people refuse to repent and many perish. God's will has not taken place.

*The Lord is not slack concerning His promise, as some count slackness, but is longsuffering toward us, **not willing that any should perish but that all should come to repentance*** (2 Peter 3:9).

Secondly, the scripture makes it clear that sin is never the will of God.

For this is the will of God, your sanctification*: that you should abstain from sexual immorality; that each of you should know how to possess his own vessel in sanctification and honor, not in passion of lust, like the Gentiles who do not know God* (1 Thessalonians 4:3-5).

Yet, every day people sin. God's will has not taken place.

When I was a teen-ager I read a book written by a mother whose daughter was kidnapped and murdered. In the book she wrote how she believed this was the will of God for her daughter. That belief was and is - entirely and totally wrong. Murder is never the will of God. Murder is sin. God's will did not take place in this young girl's life.

Many of the tragic things we see in life which steal, kill and destroy are not the will of God. Yet, many Christians in the face of all kinds of tragedy will stand and say things like, *"God's will always takes place. This tragedy was the will of God. He has a reason that we can't understand but someday, in the sweet by and by, we will understand it all."* Numerous Christians also have a hard time staying consistent in prayer. Could it be that part of the problem is rooted in their not recognizing how essential prayer really is in order for God's will come to pass? After all, if His will always takes place, why even pray at all?

This is why; thirdly, we are advised to pray for God's will to be done on this earth. Think about it, why would he have us pray for His will to be done if it always automatically takes place?

*"In this manner, therefore, pray: Our Father in heaven, Hallowed be Your name. Your kingdom come. **Your will be done on earth as it is in heaven**"* (Matthew 6:9, 10).

It is imperative that we pray for His will to take place in our life, our family, our church, our city, our nation, our world. Here is the power of praying in tongues. With our natural mind we do not always perceive the will of God. Praying in the Spirit grants us the ability to pray out the perfect will of God, even when we are not 100% sure of what it is. It enables us to step into the future and past our present place of weakness.

43

Likewise the Spirit also helps in our weaknesses. For we do not know what we should pray for as we ought, but the Spirit Himself makes intercession for us with groanings which cannot be uttered. Now He who searches the hearts knows what the mind of the Spirit is, because He makes intercession for the saints according to the will of God (Romans 8:26, 27).

Two winters ago, my family and I were coming home from church. There was a mixture of rain and snow falling. As we began to merge onto the expressway we lost all control and swiftly executed a doughnut into the oncoming lane of traffic. We were in a small Honda Civic. Coming straight for my door was a pretty blue SUV. I still remember what a pretty blue color it was. Many, when they are in accidents will yell out to Jesus in prayer when they see it coming. I did not pray. I only remained perfectly calm as I watched the SUV approach. In hind sight, as I sit here thinking, I wonder if the reason I did not cry out, "Jesus, help us!" was because, through the avenue of praying in tongues, I had already covered this event to take place in our future. It was God's will for us to live and not to die. When I woke up that morning I did not know we would lose control on the expressway. I did not know a pretty blue SUV would be heading our way. This was my weakness.

God's Spirit knew. He helped me in my weakness.

The car was totaled. We were all taken to the hospital in an ambulance. We all walked out of the hospital a few hours later! This evidence is enough to inspire me. I will not quit praying in tongues, no matter how fierce the persecution against this teaching is or how much I am mocked for it. There is one thing of which I am certain, there is no safer place to be than in His perfect will. For this reason I write, in order to keep you in the center of it.

The Rejoicing

Rejoice always, **pray without ceasing,** *in everything give thanks; for this is the will of God in Christ Jesus for you.*
(1 Thessalonians 5:16-18)

Rejoice, pray always and give thanks - three clear directions in order to fulfill the will of God. We want God's will performed in our lives, right? But how do we do it - pray without ceasing? We pray in tongues.

When all I could do was pray in English, to pray for long periods of time was quite difficult for me. I would run out of things to say fairly quickly. Praying in tongues, on the other hand, has enabled me to pray and pray and pray. I pray in tongues while I am reading the Bible, making dinner, doing the dishes, blow drying my hair, driving my car, riding my bike, mowing the lawn, and even while watching television. If you will, I pray without ceasing! In fact, when I am physically too tired to pray coherently in English, I can still pray in tongues. My husband has told me, he has heard me praying in tongues even while I was sleeping!

It is easy to pray freely in the spirit even while our mind is preoccupied with the things of this life. When we pray in tongues, the Holy Spirit gives to our spirit the words to say.

Our spirit does the praying, not our mind.

*...For if I pray in a tongue, my spirit prays, but my understanding is unfruitful (*1 Corinthians 14:14).

We can even pray in tongues while we walk through a fire, including one that is so dense with smoke it makes our eyes burn.

45

Being the president of a non-profit organization has had its challenges. A common form of fire I have run into is financial. Take, for example, the day a large donor to our ministry informed me they would soon no longer be supporting us. Upon hearing this, I calmly smiled on the outside while inside my heart crashed and burned. My mind raced, *"Again? Not again."* The devil screamed, *"See, you have been wrong all these many years. It is not God's will for you to be in the ministry. This proves it. No one wants to support you because it is not the will of God!"* The smoke was burning my eyes. I wanted to cry.

Having no idea how the scorching bills of the future would be paid, I just wanted to sit there. Joy was melting away like ice on hot pavement. We were scheduled to go to our friend's house for dinner that evening. I did not want to go, not at all. Feeling emotionally drained, I wanted to simply shut down. Forcing myself to move, I proceeded to make the potato salad I was scheduled to bring that evening. As I cut the potatoes, peeled the eggs, and sliced the celery, I did something else. I prayed without ceasing... I prayed in tongues.

It wasn't long and my spirit was strengthened to such a degree I was able to see through the smoke. I saw my future, filled with hope. To sit and wallow in self- pity was no longer an option. I was ready to keep going, going forward. I smiled – inside and out. What's more, that evening at our friend's home, I not only smiled: I laughed...and laughed...and laughed.

Our spirit man is always rejoicing. When we pray in the Spirit, the joy of our spirit is recharged -recharged to such a degree it swallows the heaviness of our flesh. Our mourning is turned to dancing as our spirit takes delight. Praying in the Spirit will help us to overcome depression of every kind!

Rejoice always, pray without ceasing, in everything give thanks; for this is the will of God in Christ Jesus for you. (1 Thessalonians 5:16-18)

In everything give thanks. How do we give thanks in the fire? How do we rejoice when our eyes burn? The same way we pray without ceasing. We open our mouth and pray in the Spirit, whether we feel like it or not. Praying in this way unlocks praise from our belly that no fire can withstand. It is a rushing, mighty river.

I will praise the name of God with a song, And will magnify Him with thanksgiving (Psalm 69:30).

The Psalmist made it clear, we magnify God with thanksgiving. Magnifying something makes it appear much bigger in our eyes. Thanksgiving is important. It magnifies God to such a degree; we see how big He really is compared to the flames. The strength of the fire we walk through is actually small and incredibly weak, in comparison to the water of His Spirit. Think about it for a minute - *is it any harder for God to heal cancer than to heal a cold?* Of course not, it just seems bigger and harder in our eyes.

Has anything ever looked impossible in your eyes? This is the time to give thanks well. You will not just see Him through the smoke - *you will see Him magnified.* When we see, truly see, how big our God really is, faith will come alive. When faith comes alive, mountains move.

Look at what the Apostle Paul wrote about what happens when we pray in tongues.

For you indeed give thanks well... (1 Corinthians 14:17).

47

This is exciting. When we pray in tongues we give thanks well! Therefore, when we pray in tongues, God is magnified in our eyes. All of a sudden, it is quite obvious - *no fire is too big for God.*

I told you that a big financial donor to our ministry had informed me of their intention to discontinue support. They were, in fact, our biggest supporter of all. At least they were in my eyes...until I gave thanks well. Now, all of a sudden, God was magnified in my eyes. I could see how big He really was. He was, by far, my BIGGEST supporter. My bills were so small compared to God. My faith came alive. I smiled and kept going. I had a very big provider.

How do you thank Him for saving your soul?

How do you thank Him for moving mountains?

How do you thank Him for overcoming the fire?

How do you thank Him for joy in the morning?

How do you thank Him when human words are not enough?

 Answer: Open your mouth and pray in tongues.

For you indeed give thanks well... (1 Corinthians 14:17).

The Resistance

Satan wants us to die in the fire. He really does.

The thief does not come except to steal, and to kill, and to destroy (John10:10a).

Imagine someone attempting to flee a burning building while being shot at by terrorists who are blocking all the fire escapes. They will have a much better chance at freedom if we give them a weapon to fight back with. After all, no weapon in hand equals: no counter attack. No counter attack equals: no way of escape.

Satan abhors the gift of tongues. Why? It is a weapon in our hands - a weapon that allows us to fight back, to fight back and win. The enemy of our soul has many strategies and wiles that he raises against us, shooting at us again and again and again. What he really loves is a target that does not shoot back. Throughout the ages he has attempted to render the church weaponless by convincing untold thousands of believers that tongues is of the devil, when in reality it is a weapon that renders the plans he forms against us null and void. Since, praying in the spirit is an offensive weapon against him; he is delighted when we drop it.

*Therefore take up the whole armor of God that you may be able to withstand in the evil day, and having done all, to stand. Stand therefore, having girded your waist with truth, having put on the breastplate of righteousness, and having shod your feet with the preparation of the gospel of peace; above all, taking the shield of faith with which you will be able to quench all the fiery darts of the wicked one. And take the helmet of salvation, **and the sword of the Spirit, which is the word of God; praying always with all prayer and supplication in the Spirit** (Ephesians 6:13-18a).*

The Romans soldiers were given a two-edged sword to do battle with. Why? A two-edged sword wreaks tremendous damage to the aggressor. It was a favorite of the Roman soldiers who used them to literally gut their enemies.

We too have been given a two-edged sword to do battle with.

And take the helmet of salvation, and the sword of the Spirit, which is the word of God: praying always with all prayer and supplication in the Spirit (Ephesians 6:17,18a).

Notice the punctuation marks in the verse listed above. There is not a period between the Word of God and praying always with all prayer and supplication in the Spirit, there is a colon. Could it be that a colon is necessary in order to describe both sides of the sword of the Spirit? One edge of our sword is the living, powerful Word of God. The other side is the power of praying in the Spirit! The Word and prayer form the razor sharp sword of the Spirit that causes the enemy to flee.

Let's look at how it is worded in Young's Literal Translation.

*and the helmet of the salvation receive, and the sword of the Spirit, which is the saying of God, through all prayer and supplication **praying at all times in the Spirit** (Ephesians 6:17-18a).*

When we pray in tongues we are praying in the Spirit. All forms of prayer should be used in our fight against the enemy. However, praying in tongues is an offensive spiritual weapon that many fail to yield. They will pick up their Bible, marching forward, while leaving the seemingly foolish weapon of tongues far behind. This is definitely, not good for two reasons. Number one, it takes the double edge off the sword.

And, number two, it takes away your secret weapon. You see, praying in the spirit is not just a weapon. It is, in fact, a secret weapon. When we pray in tongues, the devil has no idea what we are praying about. **We are praying mysteries that only God knows.**

For he who speaks in a tongue does not speak to men but to God, for no one understands him; however, in the spirit he speaks mysteries (1 Corinthians 14:2).

Satan, the prince of this world, can never comprehend the mysteries we speak forth by the spirit. If Satan could have understood the mysteries of God, he never would have had Christ crucified. That is for sure.

However, we speak wisdom among those who are mature, yet not the wisdom of this age, nor of the rulers of this age, who are coming to nothing. But we speak the wisdom of God in a mystery, the hidden wisdom which God ordained before the ages for our glory, which none of the rulers of this age knew; for had they known, they would not have crucified the Lord of glory (1 Corinthians 2:6-8).

The things of the Spirit can never be understood by natural man. How much more handicapped are Satan and his cohorts at discerning the things of the spirit, in particular this gift of the spirit called tongues? It must drive him crazy not to know what we are speaking!

The unspiritual man does not receive the gifts of the Spirit of God, for they are folly to him, and he is not able to understand them because they are spiritually discerned (1 Corinthians 2:14/ Revised Standard Version).

The interpretation of tongues is a gift of the Holy Spirit - a gift Satan does not possess. At times he counterfeits the gifts of the Spirit but, it is impossible for him to truly operate in them. We can see this when we look at psychic predictions, a good counterfeit at times, but often inaccurate. Satan can never flow in the pure gift of prophecy. The true gift of prophecy is only of the Spirit. So also, the true gift of interpreting tongues is only of the Spirit. God understands what we are praying when we speak in tongues. Sometimes, through the gift of interpretation, we understand what we are praying. Satan, however, never understands and this is good thing. We are praying heavenly strategies that he is powerless to stop because he is absolutely clueless as to what they are!

Is it beneficial for a military's secret battle plans to be revealed on public television? Of course not - broadcasting secrets makes for some pretty unsuccessful battles. In the same way, Satan does not always need to know what you are praying. When fighting the battle, it is good to keep him in the dark.

Take for example again, one of the numerous fires I have faced in regards to *Fresh Hope Ministries* in the area of finances. Great resistance was coming against us and in order for the ministry to continue, I needed to face it strong. I picked up every spiritual weapon I knew - including praying in tongues. After quite some time, the resistance broke as an individual stepped up to donate the needed finances. I did indeed, rejoice.

Looking back on this, I realize God had planned a strategy. He would speak to this particular donor and lead them by His still, small voice to help us out. What may have happened if Satan knew exactly who it was that God was planning to speak to and direct to help us out financially? Would he have left our future donor alone? Do you think he would have stayed silent and not tried to tempt them into not giving?

Oh no, he would have sent demons to speak to their heart and say things like. *"That is not God telling you to give that money. You may need it. What if there is an emergency and you don't have enough to pay all your bills? You deserve to keep it anyway. You deserve some nice things in life. You are donating money all the time. You can't give to everyone."* And maybe, just maybe, he would have been able to convince them. However, if their identity remained a secret... he would have no way of knowing who God was leading to give.

If the battle plan is secret,

the enemy does not know how to counter it!

*Therefore take up the whole armor of God, that you may be able to withstand in the evil day, **and having done all**, to stand* (Ephesians 6:13).

The Recharge

But you, beloved, building yourselves up on your most holy faith, praying in the Holy Spirit (Jude 1:20).

Did you ever feel that your faith was weak? When a battery is weak it is in need of a recharge. Our inward man requires no less. It needs a daily renewal in order to keep going when facing the fire.

Therefore we do not lose heart, even though our outward man is perishing, yet the inward man is being renewed day by day (2 Corinthians 4:16).

We have already discovered that praying in tongues builds up our inner man, our spirit man. Our spirit man is never in doubt. Our spirit man is always walking in faith. It is our flesh that doubts. It is our flesh that grows weak. Our spirit is strong enough to move a mountain.

What mountain do you currently need to move? I needed the mountain of lack to move. I spoke to the mountain just like Jesus said to. Only one thing... It did not move! There it remained, tall and proud. Its very existence was a clear sign that I had not spoken in faith. My doubting flesh was much too weak to move a mountain with roots this deep.

*"For assuredly, I say to you, whoever says to this mountain, 'Be removed and be cast into the sea,' **and does not doubt in his heart, but believes** that those things he says will be done, he will have whatever he says* (Mark 11:23).

So I spoke to my mountain again, but this time I spoke to it in tongues. All the while I was praying in the Spirit, my inner man was recharging, growing stronger, increasing in faith.

When my faith was strong, I opened my mouth and spoke again, in English this time, to my mountain. It moved! The seemingly impenetrable mountain of lack was plucked up and cast easily into the sea by the power of faith that resided in my spirit. This is why we must continue to build up our most holy faith, praying in the Spirit. It causes mountains to move!

But you, beloved, **building yourselves up on your most holy faith,** *praying in the Holy Spirit* (Jude 1:20).

The other day I noticed I was getting upset at my husband over small things in a big way. Why was I so cranky? Why was I so short fused? I thought about it. In the midst of producing a weekly television show and being a wife, mom and grandma, I had gotten so busy that I forgot to pray in tongues for a little while! It doesn't take long for my flesh man to take over when this happens. This is not good because flesh man is a crab who gets offended so easily and would rather take any walk BUT the love walk!

I definitely needed my love for my husband recharged. So, what did I do? I prayed in tongues for quite a while as I cleaned and prepared food for company. After a while my anger subsided and my love for him was strong and healthy once again. Praying in tongues recharges your love. The value of speaking in tongues, therefore, is infinite for God said the greatest is love.

And now abide faith, hope, love, these three; **but the greatest of these is love** (1 Corinthians 13:13).

Faith and love are both mentioned in the above scripture. They are linked together again when the Apostle Paul reveals that only faith that works through love avails.

For in Christ Jesus neither circumcision nor uncircumcision avails anything, but **faith** **working through love** (Galatians 5:6).

The Apostle Jude puts faith on one side, love on the other and praying in the Spirit in the middle!

*But you, beloved, building yourselves up on your most holy **faith**, **praying in the Holy Spirit**, keep yourselves in the **love** of God* (Jude 1: 20, 21a).

We all want our faith to flow through the conduit of love; after all, if we have faith that moves a mountain and don't have love it profits nothing. So, maybe, just maybe, those who are short on faith that is motivated by love are forgetting something very important. To pray in tongues on a consistent basis!! The benefits of praying in the Spirit seem endless. They really do. It can even, for example, help to recharge your memory!

My friend and ministry partner, Bill Lynch, is full of a great love for God and a true zest for life. Sometimes, however, in his zeal, he tends to forget things. His wife will agree with me on that! It is a good thing that Bill speaks in tongues. He has told me that often, when he does lose something such as his car keys, he prays in the Spirit and - all of a sudden he remembers right where he laid them! I know what he means. I have had the same thing happen to me more than once.

*"But the Helper, the Holy Spirit, whom the Father will send in My name, He will teach you all things, **and bring to your remembrance** all things that I said to you* (John 14:26).

*Likewise the Spirit also **helps in our weaknesses**. For we do not know what we should pray for as we ought, but the Spirit Himself makes intercession for us with groanings which cannot be uttered* (Romans 8:26).

I have had the Holy Spirit remind me of important things at just the right time causing me to avoid more than one disaster! To say that He helps in my weakness is an understatement.

Speaking of weakness, do you ever feel weak, weary, or just plain worn out? Praying in the Spirit is vital for you. It brings rest to the weary. When I am physically, emotionally and spiritually worn out I find refreshing (spirit, soul and body) by praying in tongues.

I have had times when I preached multiple services in a row. Sometimes, after all the preaching was done, I felt like a limp dish rag. Tired and physically worn out. It would sometimes take me a significant amount of time to get my energy back again. Until, I discovered the truth that praying in tongues could refresh me! Now, when this happens, I recharge myself by praying in the Spirit. After the service is all done I just open up my mouth, in the middle of my hotel room, and pray in tongues. My tiredness flees and I am able to go about my life immediately, whereas in the past I needed a day or more to just rest and get my strength back again.

For with stammering lips and another tongue he will speak to this people, to whom he said, "This is the rest with which You may cause the weary to rest," and "THIS IS THE REFRESHING!" (Isaiah 28:11-12a).

When we minister and serve out of our spirit for a significant amount of time, it is important to refuel, strengthen and refresh our spirit man once again. Spiritual burnout can be avoided when we take the time to edify ourselves in this manner. How can one become spiritually dry when rivers of living water are flowing from his belly?

The Recall

Let us take a minute and recall some of the wonderful things we receive as we pray in tongues.

-the perfect will of God

-rest

-refreshing

-power

-strength

-the ability to give thanks well

-our spirit man built up

-things brought to our remembrance

-the enemy defeated

-a greater walk of love

-the ability to overcome the fire

These are just a few of the things we have discussed. For the sake of time I will not list every single benefit of speaking in tongues that we have covered thus far. If I were to keep on studying and writing, I could probably find more and more of the benefits of this gift to teach you. For every gift that God gives is multi-faceted. Yet, I feel it is time to be done, to add only one last chapter. It is time to release this book. Why? Someone is waiting to receive the gift of a new language.

Is it you?

The Receiving

If you have already received the gift of praying in tongues then I would like you to pray this prayer with me...

Dear Father God,

I thank you for the gift of praying in tongues. It is a precious gift with infinite value. I regret any time or ways that I have taken this precious gift for granted and not valued it as I should. I ask you to help me, with the grace and power of Your Spirit, to remember to pray in tongues on a consistent basis.

In Jesus Name, Amen!

If you have not yet received the gift of praying in tongues but would like to, I would like to lead you in a pray as well. But first, let me explain something very important to you. When you pray in tongues, your spirit (not your mind) does the praying.

*For if I pray in a tongue, **my spirit** prays, but my mind is unfruitful* (1 Corinthians 14:14).

You see, an individual can pray in tongues while their mind is preoccupied with something else. You can pray in tongues and do the dishes, wash the car, dry your hair or even put on make-up. I even pray in tongues while I read the Bible. It is easy to do because when we pray in tongues our mind is not praying but our Spirit is. Notice again, it clearly says that when I pray in a tongue **my spirit** prays. Because it is YOUR spirit, YOU have to open your mouth and start to say something.

It is not going to shoot out of you like vomit!

God is not going to reach His hand down from heaven and start flapping your jaws. He will never force you to do anything. God is a gentleman. Therefore, He allows you to choose when to pray in the Spirit and when not to. The exact same way that He allows you to choose when to start praying in English, is the same way that He allows you to choose when to start praying in tongues. Yes, the Holy Spirit does give our spirit the utterance, (the words to say) but it is our spirit that does the praying. The choice is yours. It is according to your will. So do what Paul did and say, "I will pray with the spirit!"

What is the conclusion then? **I will pray with the spirit,** *and I will also pray with the understanding. I will sing with the spirit, and I will also sing with the understanding* (1 Corinthians 14:15).

You do not need to wait for a goose bump or until you reach a certain level of spiritual maturity. I knew a lady who thought she could only pray in tongues when a certain emotional feeling or spiritual high came upon her. Some people think you can only pray in tongues if you are especially good and holy. These things are not true according to the Word of God. The Bible clearly describes tongues as a gift of the Spirit. You do not earn a gift, you receive it. All of God's gifts are received by grace, not by works. God would have ALL His children speak in tongues. It is his will for all His children because He is a good God. He knows how much **every one** of us needs this gift.

*I would like **every one** of you to speak in tongues*
(1 Corinthians 14:5).

I encourage you to wait no longer. There are only two simple steps to take in order to pray in tongues.

1. Ask the Holy Spirit to fill you
2. Open your mouth and begin

Are you ready- ready for a recharge? Pray the following prayer in order to be filled with the Holy Spirit and then... open your mouth and begin. Pray in a language that changes everything.

Your life will never be the same.

Dear Father God,

I thank you so much for the gift of your Holy Spirit. You said that all I need to do to receive the fullness of Your Spirit is to ask. So right now I ask you to fill me with Your Holy Spirit. From the top of my head, to the tip of my toes may I be completely immersed, filled, and baptized with the Holy Spirit. I want all of the Holy Spirit that I can possibly have and all of the gifts He gives. I receive the gift of speaking in tongues right now. I will now open my mouth and speak in tongues and as I do I am being recharged, refreshed, strengthened and made ready to fulfill all your will and purpose for my life and to further the advancement of the kingdom.

In Jesus Name, Amen!

A Cordial Invitation

I would like to cordially invite you to visit my website at www.myfreshhope.com in order to view my weekly television program entitled, My Fresh Hope.

I pray you find there, fresh hope for a new day!

Sincerely,
Sally Ro

Printed in Great Britain
by Amazon